PRINCIPLES OF
SMALL BUSINESS

Principles of Small Business

A Look at Critical Components for Small Business Success

Kieran Mohammed

To order additional copies of this book, contact:
Xlibris LLC
1-888-795-4274
www.Xlibris.com
Orders@Xlibris.com
139239

CONTENTS

PREFACE

This book is designed to assist the small-business owner and entrepreneur with decision making and principle building in order to successfully start and run a small business. It applies decision-making analysis and demonstrates the value of four critical principles: process, strategy, financial intelligence (business economics and financial analysis), and ethics and concisely explains their value to the small-business owner. The language is simple and straightforward, with no requirement for prior experience or business sense. It is written to assist the individual passionate about their product or service but not acquainted with the technicalities of business ownership or the current business owner or manager struggling to overcome hurdles preventing growth and inflating cost.

It provides useful definitions, comparisons, and rationale that will allow the entrepreneur and small-business owner to understand the concepts and principles needed to establish a successful business.

One of the key components to keep in mind when you read this book is the mental approach with which you will be perceiving the information. This book seeks to engage the reader and begin the thought process. If you are already an established small-business owner *or* if you already have an established small business, your thought process should be more directed to business growth and success and, therefore, toward process improvement and strategy; and if you are an entrepreneur, you will value the decision-making features and mental-preparation aspects within these pages as well as the process, strategy, ethics, and financial intelligence components. This book will be valued by the first time small-business owner, entrepreneur, middle and upper management, as well as students, and those who have plateaued or are struggling to transition from the *survival* to the *success* phase of business and are in need of simple, affordable guidance.

SMALL-BUSINESS SUCCESS

It is not easy to turn a vision or dream into reality. There are core concepts and principles involved with starting, growing, and maintaining a small business successfully. Anyone with sufficient financing can start a business in theory, and many take the chance practically, only to run into decision-making and business-management hindrances. It takes an understanding of critical business principles such as process, strategy, financial intelligence, and ethics to do it successfully.

From a financial perspective, in its most basic form, a business can be explained as simply using money to make money. From a strategic perspective, small business can be getting from where you are to where you want to be. From a process perspective, a small business can be a series of steps performed to generate revenue. From an ethical standpoint, it can be a way to bring needed goods and services to the community.

The *success* of a small business is based on the various components of how efficient you can continuously produce, market, and sell your product or service. From these perspectives, it is important to understand that owning and running a business are demanding and rewarding. Take this comparison for example: the top percentile of wealth in the world belongs to entrepreneurs; however, most of those in the working world are employees. Entrepreneurship does not provide the security of the corporate world. It does not come with the established entity or the organizational culture. All this has to be built. It is the requirements of nurturing a business from start-up to growth to maturity that make small-business ownership both rewarding and challenging.

People start business for various reasons but always for the intent of making money. The reality of small-business ownership is that most that got into small-business ownership were not prepared to be small-business owners. They had the skill or the talent or the financing to start a business and were seeking to exploit that to generate revenue but had no process, strategy, or realistic vision of getting the desired result. A business built on poor process can recover, but a business established on poor principle will fail.

If the entrepreneur is going to succeed in small-business ownership, he needs to understand the fundamentals needed for success in the small-business world. He needs to understand process, strategy, financial intelligence, and ethics and their applications.

UNDERSTANDING THE CAUSE OF SMALL-BUSINESS FAILURE

If you're going to succeed in small-business ownership, you must understand what causes failure. Owning a business requires more goals from the entrepreneur than effectively securing the start-up funding. You must efficiently be able to identify and address those areas that will affect your business's success. There will continuously be ways to improve process and strategy in order to succeed; and as such, as a small-business owner, you must be able to adjust your processes and strategy in an ethical and financially sound manner. As technology advances, processes and strategy will surface that will allow for expansion into dimensions not previously explored. However, the principles of success will remain the same.

Many of today's small businesses are failing at an alarming rate and have adopted a survival approach rather than one built for success. It is estimated that 50 percent of small businesses fail within five years. With all the small-business resources available today, why is this such an epidemic?

It is imperative that the entrepreneur enters the business realm mentally prepared with a sound process and strategy for the start and the short-term future. Short term for a new small-business owner suggests the next twelve to thirty-six months. Anticipation of hurdles and an assessment of the business terrain are critical components of the initial planning process. To successfully navigate this course, the entrepreneur or small-business owner must be competent and a jack-of-all-trades seemingly. He must be a wizard almost to the point where he can foresee the future and make moves in anticipation of the forthcoming ebbs and flows of the market in order to gain the best leverage. It seems almost like a fantasy approach, or is it just a matter of process and strategy planning?

Big businesses have been applying strategy, financial analysis, and processes to do just that. What is it that segregates these successes from the small businesses that fail? size? capital? resources? Logically, it seems that the handicaps of a big business should be the advantages of a small business, and both should have leverage to balance the other and share market space. It's in the details of functionality and principles that we find the answer. Today's small-business owner is too focused with *fast* money as the mission while the larger firms are built on longevity and leverage for market space. The small-business owners of today are making more and more irrational decisions based on emotion and desperation and what they see others doing rather than on process and strategy. They find themselves with high employee-turnover rates, inefficient processes, poor strategy for success, and avoiding ethics as a cost-saving strategy.

While the small-business owner is thinking about making more money, the larger firms are thinking about gaining more customers and market share and the criteria that affect that. In essence, they are both focused on the same goal, but the strategy and process of them getting there are what make all the difference. The larger entities see the direct relation between customer satisfaction, employee satisfaction, growth, and revenue *and* act upon that relation while the small-business owner goes directly at the financial approach, usually causing them to miss the opportunity, devalue their product or service, or miss the goal altogether.

Once you realign the focus correctly, you realize that it's the intent of the small-business owners, their own mission, and their goal setting of simply making money that are causing their demise. Nothing is wrong with the concept of making money—it is why the business world exists; however, it is the approach and the application of this concept that create an issue. Is making money the goal or the mission?

The small-business owner starting with the wrong mentality is like venturing on a great trip with the wrong map. Small businesses are started more with financial-oriented decisions than with process and strategy. The small-business owners today get into business because they can afford to. So they get started by being focused on the financial start-up alone and hope to succeed.

That's like having a weight-loss goal and buying the pills or the meals or the gym membership and thinking that is sufficient.

One simple approach is to bring the big-business *success mentality* to the small-business owners along with some of the tools that will be effective in the small-business market. Of course, this mentality and tool set needs to be repackaged to present value and compatibility to the small-business arena. This book endeavors to apply that repackaging to accommodate today's small-business owner. The mentality of the small-business owner has to be focused on attaining and retaining customers, or *market share* as the big firms refer to this. When applying decision making, there is a tool already in existence in journalism and legal review process that small-business owners are definitely aware of and can harness to effectively make decisions. You might have heard of the *five* W*s* *and one* H, or the who, what, why, when, where, and how.

If small-business decisions are made by implementing these six questions, this tool will serve to slow down your thought process to consider all the various dimensions of the decision-making process. This is important in small-business decision making. The discipline is that you need to make time for this decision-making process and understand how critical it is to your success as a small-business owner.

Principles of Business Functionality

BusinessDictionary.com defines *principles* as "fundamental norms, rules, or values that represent what is desirable and positive for a person, group, organization, or community, and help it in determining the rightfulness or wrongfulness of its actions. Principles are more basic than policy and objectives, and are meant to govern both" and defines *goal* as "an observable and measurable end result having one or more objectives to be achieved within a more or less fixed timeframe."

It is important for business owners to understand the difference between principles and goals. Your business will be defined by your principles that you establish, and the goals you set must be in compliance with those principles.

When it comes to the other areas of functionality and execution of decisions and ideas, the focus should be heavily weighted on the principles of customer satisfaction and value, utilizing the tools of process, strategy, and financial intelligence. All these tools should be governed by ethics. You want to ensure your process, strategy, and financial intelligence are implemented and performed ethically for the sake of the business, customer, community, and cost.

Some examples of simple tools to be able to have a working knowledge to assist in this preparation are the following:

For financial intelligence:

- A budget
- Business economics reports (micro and macro)
- Financial statements, such as balance sheets, income statements, and profit and loss

Strategy and process applications such as the following:

- Strength, weakness, opportunity, and threat analysis (SWOT)
- Root-cause analysis tools that include process mapping, fishbone diagrams
- Simple histograms for gauging production and usage

Ethical practices such as these:

- Proper business documentation, such as licenses and permits
- Record keeping and qualified staff
- Policy and procedure manuals

These tools and the understanding of their purpose and function in a small business would help you to lay out the initial road map called your business plan and guide you in making successful decisions and achieving the overall mission of making money. These simple tools will assist in resolving many of the cost and performance issues you will encounter as a small-business owner. Best of all, you can apply these tools with pen and paper if you wish—extremely cost-effective.

CRITICAL COMPONENTS IN ACTION

Let's look at a brief analysis of traditional storefront cell phone service providers: business-functionality proof of the effect of process, strategy, financial intelligence, and ethics.

Cell phone contracts seem very complicated, and many sales contracts are written in that manner purposely because the cell phone sales are in a fairly fast-moving environment. Proper perusal and understanding of the contract terms may take a few hours at least, and you may have questions that the sales representatives are not in the position to answer. For example, if you were to ask a salesperson about the exclusive remedy clause in a contract, they may not be able to provide any more information than what is already written.

While taking the time to read a cell phone contract and digesting the parameters of the contract may help you decide if a plan is actually right for you, the real reason you probably went to the vendor was the phone or the cost/service of your current carrier. The businesses in this industry are aware of the business market for these products, and they devise their marketing strategy around displays and products to target these values to the customer.

After all, you don't see the contracts' and plans' details on display when you walk in the stores, right? Even with those prepaid plans available, there is still the marketing strategy of pairing a plan with more tech-savvy and eye-catching phones while the terms and conditions to agree to in order to receive those services take a backseat.

The process that cell phone providers use is simple and effective. The eye candy and technology of the cell phones are displayed with accessibility, allowing you to utilize your senses, thereby playing to your emotion; and they are offered at a price point designed to be attractive and of value.

The service providers make many times over the cost they incurred through the monthly plan, and they know how to ensure they make their forecasted sales by implementing certain parameters, such as a two-year agreement with an early termination penalty or, in the no-contract services, markup of the up-front price of the phone and reduction of the accessibility of the additional features of a contractual plan. But where is the ethics in all this? Seemingly, I have pointed out adverse ethical practice in the overall scheme of marketing.

The ethics is covered in the contract that you sign or in the terms and conditions of the prepaid plan. We are not focusing on the ethics of the sales staff but rather on the ethics involved in the overall strategy and process. Sometimes the contract may come in electronic format; you know that box that you need to check "I Agree" that you scroll to the bottom area to sign? That's you agreeing to the compliance, policy, and regulations aspects, which make all this ethical, provide parameters for you to abide by, and protect the vendor. So you see how effective their process, financial intelligence, ethics, and strategy work; and the cell phone industry is one that seems unaffected by the economy even though specific components' sales—such as phone brands—seem to ebb and swell with the economy. The service providers themselves have created a seemingly economy-proof market.

Yet if we look at recent occurrences in the cell phone industry, we see that some companies rose and others fell. What impacted this rise and fall when all carriers seemed to have competitive models and similar plans? Was it all about price?

At the end of the day, service boils down to customer satisfaction—which service was dependable in certain areas, who gave more value for the cost, etc. These fundamentals are consistent with the approach outlined in this book. Implement tools that promote quality in your process and product, spend time to devise an effective strategy that provides customers with value, ensure your price point promotes value as well as revenue, and make sure all components are ethically practiced, and you will attain market share and longevity. Focus on building market share, not making money.

The small-business owner or entrepreneur should comprehend how the interaction between decision making and understanding of the philosophies and tools of process, strategy, ethics, and financial intelligence are essential to be able to start, develop, and successfully maintain a small business. Tools by themselves cannot get the job done. You will need to be an integral part of your business's success. You will need to dedicate time, effort, resources, and revenue.

Pearls of Wisdom

- You get into business to make money—that's the *mission*.
  Think about a soldier in charge of extracting someone behind enemy lines. The extraction of the person is the mission, but the goals of that mission are what make the mission successful and of value—go in unnoticed, utilize proper equipment and personnel, bring everyone back alive, get it done in under two hours, infiltrate at night, etc.

- Your business *goal* is to provide a quality product or service.
  In business, the goals are what you, the business owner, are focused on. Setting simple and realistic goals using the process, strategy, financial intelligence, and ethics principles will simplify and organize your thought process and make goal setting, establishment, and enforcement more manageable.

- The customer is the boss; the customer can fire everyone by taking their business elsewhere (Sam Walton). The quality you put in your product or service is the value it has to the customer.
  If your product or service does not provide a value to the customer, you are not going to stay in business for too long. Your service, product, policies, and procedures must have customer value built in in order to secure a long-term relationship.

- The only thing that's constant is *change*.
  Today's small business must be able to adapt and conform efficiently to market changes. Remember a while back when pagers were all the rage? Business owners must embrace change instead of fight it. Business owners, employees, and processes must be developed to be able to adapt.

- Embrace technology; it is the most underused asset (primarily due to cost).
  Technology is an asset that can create market share for you in itself. More customers turn to websites and social media for guidance on purchasing and purchasing itself. Then they use this same technology to provide feedback, etc. If you do not harness these powerful outlets of marketing, you will handicap yourself. In the process aspect, technological tools can assist you with becoming efficient and more capable. I agree that it can be quite costly, but your financial intelligence analysis will help you decide if the investment is worth the risk.

- Time is the only resource you cannot get back—don't waste it.
  Crucial to anyone is time. Yet more of it is wasted than any replaceable resource is. Time management is a key component of efficiency; efficiency itself is a key product of lean process, and lean process is designed to cut productivity waste and reduce cost. So if we remove the middle components, we get the age-old business cliché of time = money.

- "Begin with the end in mind" (Stephen Covey).
  This is just common sense. If you don't know where you're going, then how would you know if you're on the right path? You need to have more than hope. You need to have a plan and a strategy to execute that plan. Hope is not a strategy. Your business plan and your budget are tools that you should use as a compass to gauge your course to your destination.

- "Attitude is a little thing that makes a big difference" (Winston Churchill).
  If you say "I hope," then you are leaving things to chance; but if you say "I will," then you are making a statement of action. A statement of action is extremely important for a business owner and entrepreneur, or else he becomes the owner of wishes and desires and nothing more. Your attitude as a business owner transcends your business, and you should take that as a serious responsibility if you are to succeed.

- What is possible? What you will.
  If you persevere hard enough, you will attain your goals. You hear many consultants talk about this effect where you want certain things

and, somehow, the universe aligns you up with them. Well, I believe it is your actions that line you up with those elements that you desire, but it starts with you; you must begin with the sincere "I will" statements.

- Good things happen when planned; bad things happen on their own. Things fall apart when not planned properly—plain and simple.

- Less is more.
  I hesitated to include this one, because I envisioned every procrastinator reading this with a smile. What this means is, don't overthink, overprocess, or overprepare, because then you begin to become rigid in your business structure; and referring to the bullet above regarding change, you need to have outlets and avenues to accommodate change built into your processes, systems, and strategies. The philosophy here is like building such a disaster-proof safe that you left out the door because it was a way in.

- "Everything should be made as simple as possible but not simpler" (Albert Einstein).
  Well, if Einstein said it, I am not going to try to explain it; but think of his statement with the application of value and quality and you'll see one way of how to apply this to your small business. Another good quote for the business owner from Einstein is "The same mentality that causes a problem cannot be used to solve the problem."

The Human Element and Decision Making

All the tools of success will not be of benefit unless proper decision making is applied, and thus, the human element and the role it plays in attaining success must be explored.

It starts with you, the business owner. Why do you want to start a business? Is the decision driven by the right motives? Only you can answer these questions. Even though the banks, partners, and investors may ask these questions and you'll google the perfect response for them to get the loan, etc., the caveat is "To thine own self be true."

Forcing yourself into an emotional decision will put you at a severe disadvantage in that you may not be approaching this challenge with the right mind-set. Remember, there is a lot of risk involved in the business ownership decision. Are you getting into business because you hate your current job and would like to just make the same money you are making at your corporate job by running your own business instead of working for that *savage* of a boss? Let's run with that idea. Say, you make $50,000/year, and you want to make $50,000 by baking cupcakes.

Okay, you want to earn $50,000. What does it cost to make $50,000? Before you can make your first commercially produced cupcake, you need a business license and food inspection license, a location, and possibly, staff. There are your fixed assets: machinery, location, management salary, etc. Now what about variable assets or the assets that change as the volume of production changes: hourly wages, raw materials, finished product packaging, etc.? Then there's marketing, taxes, insurance, and—you get the idea. So in order for you to make $50,000 of retained income, you may need to actually make about $100,000 in sales—that's a lot of cupcakes!

Human beings are emotional beings first and logical decision makers second. We can be disasters to our business efforts with nothing to blame besides our natural emotions and desires. This works for you as the business owner in the marketing strategy, but it can work against you in processes and other business decision-making areas.

Estimates from a local (Dover, Delaware), public-volunteer, small-business counselor suggest about 85 percent of clients that approach them about small business are not ready to start a small business, 20 percent of those that are ready actually complete the process, and less than 5 percent of those that complete the process are successfully in operation after five years. What does this actually mean? Well, if you started with one hundred potential small-business candidates, only fifteen would actually be ready to start a new business. Of that fifteen, only three would actually complete the process, and approximately one (it's actually 0.15) is successful.

Most businesses will spend about 30-33 percent of time/earnings on fixing problems and correcting errors (QI Macros consultant).

Fifty percent of all new businesses fail in their first five years (SBA.gov).

Business-Failure Theories and Today's Businesses

Michael Ames, author of *Small Business Management* (Ames and Wellsfry 1983), gave the following reasons in his book back in 1983. Let's see how they apply to today's business and what tools or areas of the process, strategy, financial intelligence, and ethics may apply:

1. Lack of experience (inability to implement proper process, strategy, and business economics)

    I would adjust this in the context of this book to focus on the lack of experience to make proper decisions. You may have had four years of culinary school and make a mean cupcake, but that's not the experience I want to focus on here. The planning, strategy, and business economics knowledge will be essential in the proper decision making. Every business owner needs to make decisions; these decisions will impact the business. It is imperative that you recognize the need for time and process in decision making to ensure you make the right decisions. Sometimes, knowing what you don't know is the key to actually making the right choices. Making decisions on emotional whim is a key attribute that lack of experience demonstrates.

2. Insufficient capital (business economics)

    Traditionally, you needed capital (money); but as of recent, you are quite aware that businesses such as Facebook and UPS had very humble beginnings. Ideas sell big in today's market, and capital can be controlled to a certain point by proper planning and strategy. There are many ways to get started in today's business world; but more important, I think, is the ability to continue to generate income, especially to hit that critical break-even point of which you should have predetermined as part of your business plan. Insufficient capital is a result of poor planning and financial intelligence. If you do not clearly outline your costs, you may find yourself making desperate decisions to complete projects. You may find yourself making poor decisions to meet overhead costs and soon incapacitate your business. Your business plan should be a *realistic* outline of your business. Have someone proofread your business plan to ensure you are not setting yourself up to fail. The Small Business Administration's SCORE program and other similar organizations may have counselors that can provide this review for little or no cost to you.

3. Poor location (strategy, business economics)
    Location, depending on the business, can be everything. It is extremely important to your cost and your strategy to pick a location that will promote sales. A sandwich shop at the side of a superhighway is probably not going to do as well as one near a lot of foot traffic in an urban, downtown area.
    Technology has made it possible to facilitate markets that were otherwise unreachable. Is this something that should be considered? Is the need for location really as important? It depends on the product or service you provide. A key decision in business planning is to identify and understand the demographic that you will serve. How does this demographic value the service or product you provide, and how does the implementation of technology affect that? Location can affect logistics in other ways that impact your business costs. Take for example the shipping of raw materials and finished products and the accessibility of raw materials. Think about the restaurant business and how important it is for chefs and owners to have access to the freshest ingredients. The benefit of this is that the customer is willing and expecting to pay the price associated with the better quality of product. In this scenario, location makes a huge impact on availability and revenue.
    What about a product such as software? You can set up shop in the middle of nowhere and all you need is Internet accessibility and defer to "the cloud." You are basically a license salesperson selling licenses to access your software, and you need a website, Internet traffic, and the ability to process electronic payments and safely transfer information. In this case, the physical location is not really a factor.

4. Poor inventory management (process)

    Here's another cost factor that proper process implementation can curb. Setting cycle counts and taking frequent assessments of inventory need and gauging sales against inventory stock-keeping units will help you control cost. This is especially important if you are considering a food industry business. Inventory management is not just limited to the finished product. You should use inventory management to gauge raw-material consumption. It can be used to determine where a process needs to be repaired or where a cost needs to be reevaluated. More importantly, this one measure can identify and pinpoint process waste. A simple implementation of a cycle count and a running record of the figures can provide insight on how your process and product use resources. It is also going to help you understand how your product moves off the shelf and allow you to understand your customer needs.

5. Overinvestment in fixed assets (business economics, ethics, strategy, process)

    This goes back to the emotional spending when addressing business needs. Yes, you need a laptop, but do you really need the computer with i7 with all the bells and whistles to run QuickBooks? Probably not. This is where you need to have that emotional control. Leave the office with items researched with your management team on a list complete with price and, yes, coupons, discount codes, etc. Your business funds should be reserved for working capital and investments with immediate cash value. As an entrepreneur or small-business owner, seek out local garage sales and open-item sales. When the critical initial stages of a business are at hand, it is vital to have operating capital over high-end fixed assets. Whatever you need to effectively get the job done is sufficient. The fulfillment of a nice executive desk with a luxurious leather executive chair sounds great and gives you, the new business owner, that sense of pride and prominence. Instead, set goals to reward yourself with these items as you hit milestones. For example, once you have attained the first ten thousand of net profit from your business's sales, then the next two thousand you make is yours to get that desk and chair. Spend responsibly and learn to become a logical, process and strategy oriented business decision maker rather than an emotional one.

6. Poor credit arrangements (business economics, ethics)
Payday loans, car title loans, lottery—all bad decisions as a business owner. You need to understand what APR (annual percentage rate) means and what the fine print in your credit card contracts say. Yes, the document behind the nice new plastic with the Visa logo on it is the contract. Turn it around and read the barely visible part. Call up the credit card company right away and ask why you got that APR and when and how it can be lowered, and *put a limit of 30 percent usage* on your card immediately. Do not jeopardize your personal credit for business transactions. Do not use your business card for personal items—that is unethical, and you are basically stealing from your business.

7. Personal use of business funds (ethics)
The conclusion of the last point flows right into this one. Do not use your business cards for personal use. Again, learn to be disciplined. A $2,500 business card cannot be turned into $25,000 by your business if you spend it on personal items. Also, there is a great breach of ethics and penalties associated with this type of usage. Not to mention, by violating the terms of the contractual agreement with the credit card company, you are committing fraud.

8. Unexpected growth (strategy, process)
On an upside, you had more than a successful start; but on the downside, you were not prepared. And why not? The purpose of the business was to make money, and the goal was to provide quality, so why the frown? Too big, too fast? Demand greater than supply? Now there are ways to control this. For example, you can raise the cost of your goods or services to control the pull effect by the market and work to reengineer your process to meet the demand. You may seek a partner whereby you supply the turnkey for a perpetual royalty or even outsource for a while. There is no business issue that there isn't a strategy to overcome. This is a problem nine out of ten business owners would prefer to have, right?
It is important to identify the real problem with uncontrolled growth. The uncontrollability extends to every aspect of the organization and may force you to spiral out of control. In other words, an unexpected growth spurt may send your small business into chaos, which will break down your processes and derail your strategy. You will spend more time and money putting out fires instead of managing the growth. Pull your team together and utilize a commonly overlooked

process tool—the calendar. Focus on the time ahead and not on the time that was lost. Assign work by level of importance and priority and communicate with your customers. Offer incentives to customers willing to work with you on time. You may want to seek a local temporary staffing agency to assist you with additional staff if needed or increase operation hours with bonus incentives, etc.

Gustav Berle adds two more reasons in *The Do-It-Yourself Business Book*.

9. Competition (strategy)

Here's another traditional citation. Firstly, you must strategize how you are going to compete, but you can only gauge the existing competition. In this context, we are going to focus on unknown competition. What if you were the barbecue king of the town and, suddenly, another pit master moved into town with a more flavorful blend? What do you do? Why compete? Seek what's called a blue ocean. More on this can be found in the book called *Blue Ocean Strategy* (Kim and Mauborgne 2005). A blue ocean is basically an unchartered market territory. Think about Cirque du Soleil, whereby circus and theater morphed to establish a new dimension from a dying market of traditional circus. Another way to deal with competition is to up the quality bar. Remember Business 101—adding quality = adding value. Therefore, give the customers a reason to come to your place instead of the competition's. A more everyday example is a gas station with a convenience store. Gas is the necessity, and why not grab a cup of Joe? You're already there pumping gas, right? So the condiment sales are boosted by the need to put gasoline in the vehicle.

10. Low sales (strategy, process, ethics)

Low sales are your fault as the business owner—plain and simple. Marketing and sales have so many avenues today, from social media to the traditional newspaper to sales seminars and hosted events to sample giveaways and competition. One of the unwritten functions of a business owner is to continue to generate leads (potential sales) and be able to close a potentially high percentage of those leads. There is an industry built around marketing and sales, so if you are posing this argument, I can show you the reason with a mirror. This is where you see whether you are of the survive or the succeed mentality. If this is the point where you start pointing at others and events around you as the faults for the lack of success, then you are showing survival traits, avoiding reality, saying it's not you but it's someone else's fault, etc. Another approach is the success approach, whereby you will confront this challenge and engage it rather than steer away from it. This action may involve hiring a commission-based sales staff or deciding to revamp your product line, rebrand yourself, and add quality, thereby increasing the value. Do market research and see if there was a market change. Why aren't you getting the projected sales figures? new product? competition? lack of quality? All solvable with a strategy and process-planning meeting. It is time to get management together with the whiteboard and markers. Don't know what to do still? Invest a few hundred dollars on a consultant.

There are many lists like the one above written throughout the years, and they vary depending on whom you ask, but there is one thing for sure. All these lists can be classified into subcategories of the topics: process, strategy, business economics, and ethics.

Negativity Leads to Failure

We must understand that we were being developed by emotion actions and poorly bred as logical thinkers from birth. However, as strategists, our strength and success was built into emotion; as children, if we wanted something, we cried, and we perfected that emotional-approach strategy throughout our childhood. As we grew older, we became more emotional buyers and more focused on our personal satisfactions, and the consequences of poor decisions were avoided or we dealt with them afterward. Whatever the case, we all became really good at using our emotions to impose our will.

As adults and entrepreneurs, we get enough money to start a business; and because we are financially positioned (or think we are), we jump into the business world to reap the benefits of small-business ownership. The fact of the matter is, you cannot take the impulses that make you a great customer and try to implement them as a business owner. However, you should apply some perspective on what makes the great customers and work back from that point to see how best to facilitate them.

Well, a great customer is one who buys and buys often, the one you know by the time and the order, the one who can say "I've been coming here for twenty years." There's no secret to the definition. Look at how much marketing today is directed toward children. Even grown-up products like cell phones, cars, and insurance are getting the kids involved, because the bottom line is that kids are great customers. They value the emotional experience and fun. If you can package that in some form, you have a hit product.

As business owners, we have to focus on who our customer will be and ensure our product, process, and strategy focus on the components that that customer base considers value. Again, the five *W*s and one *H* can help you with the due diligence.

Small-business owners today are seemingly in a rut for one reason or another. Most are still not where they want to be and have a hard time getting there. And they'll tell you why. This next section discusses some of the more frequent negativities I've heard and an elaboration on the statements.

SUCCESS OR SURVIVAL?

There is a success or survival paradigm (the internal process of interpreting reality) that we all fall into as small-business owners. Either we follow the survival paradigm, where we avoid reality, blame others, and live in denial, or we embrace reality, focus on self-improvement, and look toward success and achievement from within ourselves and, thus, follow the success paradigm. From a business management perspective, which of these describes you?

Let's take a look at some erroneous comparisons and erroneous statements derived from business-owner habits and thought processes and see if we can gain some sort of understanding as to why things are the way they are (I have placed the core concepts—process, ethics, strategy, and business economics—next to each statement to address the failed area that may have caused these statements):

- Activity = productivity (process). True or false? Why?
  False. Activity does not equal productivity. It is not uncommon to hear managers claim to be so busy yet nothing gets done. Being busy with non-value-added process is the same as wasting time. The small-business owner needs to understand that value-added activity is vitally important. For example, many local pizza stores here in the Dover, Delaware, area have pizza delivery staff available most of the time, hanging around waiting for the next delivery to be ready. Why not invest in four phone lines and have them do in-house sales or corporate sales for added commission? Have them deliver flyers to the areas they visit and save money on the mailers that may cost upward of $200 every month. Offer more pickup specials to promote pickups or do in-store giveaways, etc. I am saddened to learn that these business owners do not see the opportunity sitting around but

instead only see the overhead cost they are incurring. Again, this is due to the focus of the small-business owner, and this is a prime example of how he is defeated by his own misguidance.

- Business decision = personal decision (strategy, ethics). True or false? Why?

  False. Your personal decisions and your business decisions should never mix. You should make business decisions based on business goals and the business mission. Do you live your entire life by the business goals and the business mission? Therefore, apply the reciprocity. Your business should not be like planning a wedding or a party where every color and bow and detail needs to be how you like it. A business decision is made based on the business goals and the clients' needs. If you have the wedding or party mentality, you need to come to terms with this sooner rather than later. Would you buy a $2,000 oak desk if you had a $20,000 business credit card, or would you settle for the economical $200 IKEA desk? Depending on your answer to this question, you'll know where you are in this category. Who you are is not a bad thing. What you need to do is to understand how to control the situation. For example, if you are the hot spender, then assign the business card to a trusted manager or business partner, or ask the credit card company to set a limit of 30 percent max. Remember that credit responsibility is huge in the business world.

- Ethical approach is too expensive; we can't afford . . . (ethics, business economics). True or false? Why?

  False. Devaluating the product by using less-quality raw materials, failing to provide service as advertised, overworking good employees, and ignoring poor-performing employees are all examples not just of unethical practice but also of excellent ways to cut quality, lose good staff, and reduce clients and revenue. Small-business owners do not realize the cost of breached ethics because they do not see a direct impact on their money, but if they were to calculate the penalty for not paying employee taxes on time versus the cost of hiring a payroll firm or the rate of employee turnover and the impact it has on their overhead, they will see that little breaches of ethics add up to significant costs.

- Business is bad these days (strategy, process). Unavoidable? How?
  Part of a good, effective business plan is to prepare for the bad. When you have hit rock bottom, there's only one way you can go, so that's food for thought. However, it is more cost-effective to avoid hitting rock bottom by implementing a process-improvement strategy so you can identify the signs and act instead of react. On identifying a situation that has become undone, you need to act efficiently. Where do you turn to for help? Well, there's the Internet. Google your problem and see what pops up. Thereafter, get your management team together and do a fishbone diagram or list pros and cons of various decisions or do SWOT analysis and see what the analysis reveals as problems and avenue of potential solutions. It is times like these when you feel the need to emotionally react spontaneously that you need to slow things down and act in a logical manner. Even step away from the situation area for a while and regroup, but do not abandon the problem or turn yourself into a victim and redirect the focus.

- No one is buying; I hope things get better (process, strategy, and business economics). Right or wrong approach? Or is a business defenseless to this occurrence?
  Wrong approach. Hope is neither a strategy nor a plan. You need to go back to the survival or success paradigm and recoup yourself. Identify the shortcomings and reassess your business plan. A strength, opportunity, weakness, and threat (SWOT) analysis will lay out the picture a bit clearer and will assist in pointing you in the direction you need to go. No occurrence in business is a defenseless situation; there is always a way out and a way up. Get your team involved and share the responsibility of attaining the solution. Be open to all ideas and do not judge.

- Cutting overhead means cutting staff (strategy, process). Right or wrong? Why?
  Wrong. It's easy to fire employees and say "I'll do it myself." Then who is going to gauge the business health? Never give up employees to cut overhead; they are assets, and they can be cross-trained to increase revenue in areas such as sales and marketing. After all, they may know your products better than you do or have a social skill or ability that you don't. Employees are assets—bottom line. Your job is to train them properly and retain them as a cost-control practice. If you start the do-it-yourself approach, you will stress yourself and

those around you. Do things the right way and understand your role as a leader as well as a manager in the business-ownership position. If costs are growing, then you need to apply a process review and a financial analysis to pinpoint the areas of impact. If it turns out to be an employee, then there's training and a process review first before you should consider termination. Most employees want to work and want to do their jobs. No one gets up in the morning and goes to work with the intention of being a screwup.

- I know what's best for my business (strategy). True or false? Why? False. This is a personal, survival-paradigm-type statement that you should be aware of. It usually surfaces in those management meetings where there are conflicting opinions. Understand the consequence of this remark or mind-set. Parts of business success are employee satisfaction and client satisfaction. Even though a business might be theoretically yours, you need a team of support to succeed. Even a sole proprietor needs a customer to be successful.

- I've been doing this for *xx* years, so don't tell me how to do this (strategy, process, ethics, business economics). Right or wrong? Why? Wrong. This is closely affiliated with the previous bullet but also adds the resistance-to-change element. A successful business will be open to continuous improvement and input from staff at all levels of the organization. Just because someone does not have manager in their title, it does not mean their opinion is ineffective. Promote a team environment and a healthy organizational culture if you want to succeed.

- Business goals = business mission (strategy, process). True or false? Why? False. The biggest problem with business owners today is that they think making money is the goal, so they cut ethical and process corners, overwork and underpay employees, remove quality from products, and breach ethical requirements that benefit their employees so that they can make money to their satisfaction. Business goals are about client satisfaction, and the formula should be happy clients + happy employees = successful business owners, because if you set an environment for success, everyone will benefit and you'll get the results you seek. Goals can always change, but the mission is principle based. If the mission is set at making money, then you can adjust the goals within ethics and compliance to ensure the mission is successful. However, if you set the goal as making money, your focus becomes fine-tuned to money alone when it should be fine-tuned to client needs. This misdirection leads you to lose focus on your business environment, and soon you will encounter many areas of concern. One of the default processes of this mentality is that you select your partners, lawyers, accountants, etc., by cost rather than by quality and service.

So how do you overcome hurdles that seemingly affect every business owner? The first step is to understand that there will be hurdles to overcome. Planning is a key component, and any consultant or business assistance organization will tell you to create a business plan. Technically, a business plan is a compilation of process, strategy, business economics, and ethics and the application of the fundamental five *W*s and one *H* in all these areas. (Remember the fundamental five *W*s and one *H*: who, what, why, when, where, and how.)

PROCESS

When we think of process, we usually think of a step-by-step formula to get something done. Can process help your business to succeed? Is there a finite set of steps that you can implement as a stand-alone and sit back and watch your business succeed? The answer is most definitely *no*. Business involves human interaction; and just a perfect layout, plan, or process will not work by itself. However, a process implemented to ensure process improvement and cut productivity waste on a continuous basis will be a tremendous benefit to a start-up as long as it implements the human element. The best process is useless if it cannot be assimilated, comprehended, and executed by the human elements that it impacts. How can you implement a process? Today there are many business-process tools varying in cost, sophistication, and applicability that can be implemented at the managerial or enterprise levels. Hiring trained management can also lead to a well-established firm generated from cross-training, etc. Most efficient, though, is arming the business owner or entrepreneur with the tools and skill set to make productive decisions—a critical component for start-ups and established firms.

This is where it is important to understand the difference between management and leadership. A manager deals with a process, but a leader deals with people. A business owner must understand how to demonstrate the characteristics of the two functions. Most managers talk in terms of people when you ask them about management when, in fact, they are managing the processes that those people perform. This creates a lot of friction in today's small-business world because in a small business, the manager-employee interaction is part of the daily business function, and many managers lack the leadership skills to complement their managerial ability.

It is critical that business owners and entrepreneurs understand the need to implement a process befitting their organizational culture and capability. The simplest approach to process decision making would be to address the five *W*s and one *H*, or the who, what, why, where, when, and how.

Let's experience this from a new entrepreneur's standpoint to turn an idea into a business. The disclaimer here is that I am using an extremely basic approach and there are a lot more factors derived from the research you must perform as part of the planning process to consider and our entrepreneur has never pursued business ownership before.

So our entrepreneur has saved money and wants to open his first small business and will firstly ask *what* is needed to begin. The answer then is having a business plan to outline the idea he has. This starting point is in no way a magical revelation, but he would understand what is needed by the due diligence he should be performing on starting a new business. He may begin with *where* instead, or *why*, but the due process of exploring the five *W*s and one *H* is essential for a complete investigation into the decision-making process.

Now he addresses *how* he should perform this process, and from his research at SBA.gov or other Internet resources, he learns that there are free tools online that he can access. So in this research, he has involved the *where* and successfully addressed two of the components simultaneously.

He peruses the website and the instructions and begins the business plan but realizes that his words are not representing his thoughts correctly; he needs help. *Who* can help him? He realizes that there are many resources to creating a business plan, some at a cost and others free of charge.

Why should he choose either-or? And he goes back to research and makes a few calls and realizes that some entities are more responsive than others. He may also realize that the fee-based entities will work for his business while the free resources may require him to conform to their schedule as they are hitting a much broader market.

He now addresses *when* he needs to get this done. Is there an immediate need, or can he relax and take his time? He decides that this can be a nine-month project and he is willing to relax and take this slowly. With this time frame, he can adjust to meet the schedule of the free resources and decides to pursue those resources and then consider additional resources if he is still in need of continuous support.

By establishing the fundamental five *W*s and one *H* as a habit, he will implement a thorough thought process in decision making and is more likely to make proper, well-thought-out decisions.

Process Improvement: A Look at Some Easy-to-Implement Lean Tools

What Is *Lean*?

Lean is a synergistic approach to process whereby you get more value-driven outcomes from your process using less resources or, in other words, you remove the non-value-added steps in a process. The quality aspect of lean is that its approach is easy, simple, and continuous.

Today's business owner spends about 30 percent of time and revenue while fixing problems and correcting errors. Energy, time, and money are better served growing a business rather than repairing and troubleshooting or, as some refer to it, "putting out fires." Below are a couple of easy tools to apply that will assist you with identifying and attacking problems at their source rather than attacking the symptom. How many times have employees been blamed for working too slow, not doing a good job, wasting time, etc.? How much of this is actually the employee's fault, and how much of it is due to improper process or process guidelines? Once you address that question, ask yourself who is really to blame—the process or the person. There are many lean tools that can be implemented for process. However, the small-business owner does not need to be an expert in lean process. He needs to know how to identify problems and implement processes that are efficient. In order to do this, he may consider one of the many process tools for root-cause analysis such as fishbone diagrams.

Review of Problem Issue of Unproductivity in Postproduction Department

Packing	Picking	Shipping	Returns
Bottlenecks Why? Order buildup Why? Specialty orders requiring special packing	Temporary employees Why? Not enough pick work for staff Why? Unavailable SKUs on shelves for workers to pick Why? Packing department is backlogged	Inefficient shipping Why? Not enough stock to complete orders Why? Pick employees do not have access to SKUs by shipping due dates	High percentage of returns Why? Unhappy customers Why? Incomplete orders Why? Not enough stock on the shelves for pick workers

We can produce the processes involved in the above table in an Ishikawa, or fishbone diagram, to see where the non-value-added steps are that cause the customer dissatisfaction cited under Returns. The first thing to keep in mind is that you must prioritize your problems. In this case, you go at the one affecting your customers. Note that the Ishikawa diagram is designed to assist you with determining non-value-added steps; in other words, can you remove or improve upon a step and get the same or better results? The overall goal is to use the illustration to solve the problem at the head of the diagram. The diagram itself will not create the solution for you.

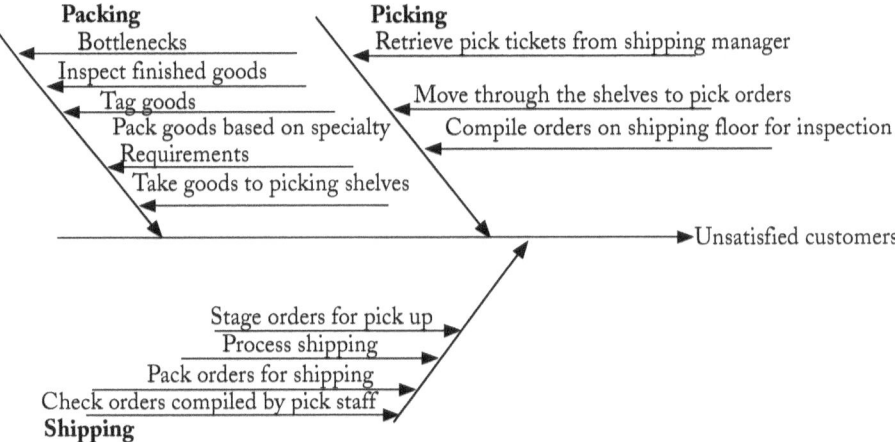

A lean tool for assisting with identifying the root cause used in process mapping to identify and eliminate non-value-added steps or productivity waste such as what has been shown in the diagram above can assist in the pinpointing of opportunity for improvement.

From the diagram, the following are noticeable:

1. The packing department and the shipping department have four steps in their processes while the picking department has just two. This is one area of opportunity for possible cross-training and implementing more productivity. We have already identified that the picking staff is underutilized and working part-time.
2. It is also visible from the diagram that the specialty work that may involve picking and sorting of specialty items coming through production may be a cross function of the packing unit that the picking unit can jump ahead of in the process and accomplish with a little reengineering of the process. To elaborate, have the picking

team pick *all* orders from the produced finished goods directly and then present them already sorted and ready for inspection, tagging, and ticket processing.

3.   Thirdly, if as a continuation of the reengineering process the packing unit will now be packing the orders for shipping, then shipping personnel can be cross-trained to stock the shelves and pack as well since they will now have to check the orders as part of the packing process instead of later on during the preparation-for-shipping phase.

There are various levels of depth that you may choose to explore with an Ishikawa diagram. The value of the tool is to present the various components of the process in one flowing, itemized format, which is easier to review.

From the Ishikawa, we can identify itemized areas of the process while viewing the entire process as a whole and allow ourselves the visibility to create more productive visibility.

There are also process-mapping functions that can be easily assimilated into the management review of process improvement. These are relatively easy ways to implement consistency into your process. More essential is the role that these simple diagrams play in assisting in identifying the root cause. Process mapping takes into account the decisions that cause an action and displays both decision and action from a starting point to an end point.

Let's take a process and map it out to see how the process-mapping diagram may be of service to the small-business owner. Let's say a consultant wants to address the response time from inquiry to response to my potential clients. From call volume to record keeping, it seems like there is lost potential for sales due to the inability to respond to customers efficiently.

We can utilize a root-cause-analysis tool called a process map to analyze the process:

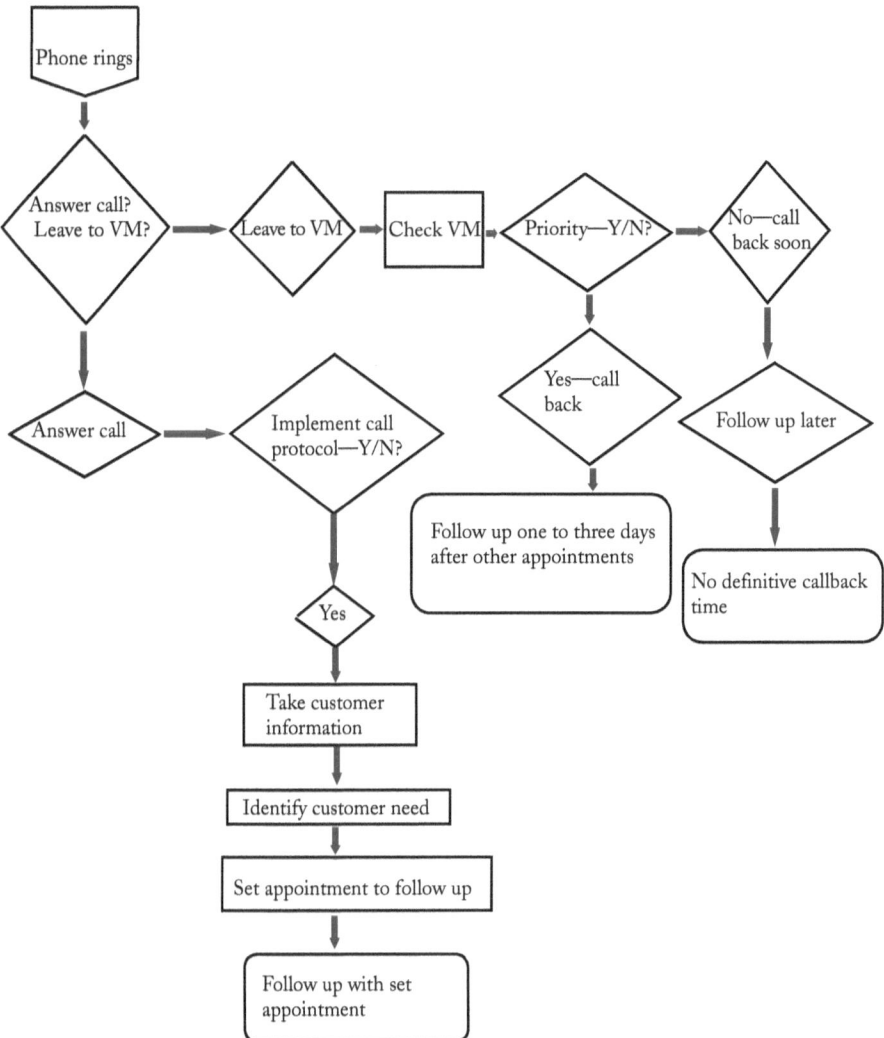

From the above diagram, you will notice that an improper process for follow-through was implemented. This type of scenario is common in small-business practice today, where only a unidirectional approach to process is implemented, leaving back doors and loopholes in the process. In this example is a great follow-up process that is "automated" and goes into effect once the phone is answered, but once a voice mail is received, the follow-up process is not as automated, allowing the consultant a response time to his satisfaction and not the customer's.

The loophole presented here demonstrates how an ineffective process can impede your business goals. By allowing the consultant and not the customer to decide the priority, a fundamental principle is broken and the process fails once a call goes to voice mail.

Another key component in the process is an organization chart. It is important to understand the role this plays in the communication hierarchy of process and the flow of process. An organization chart illustrates the hierarchy of command and communication and should be implemented into the small business with employees and management.

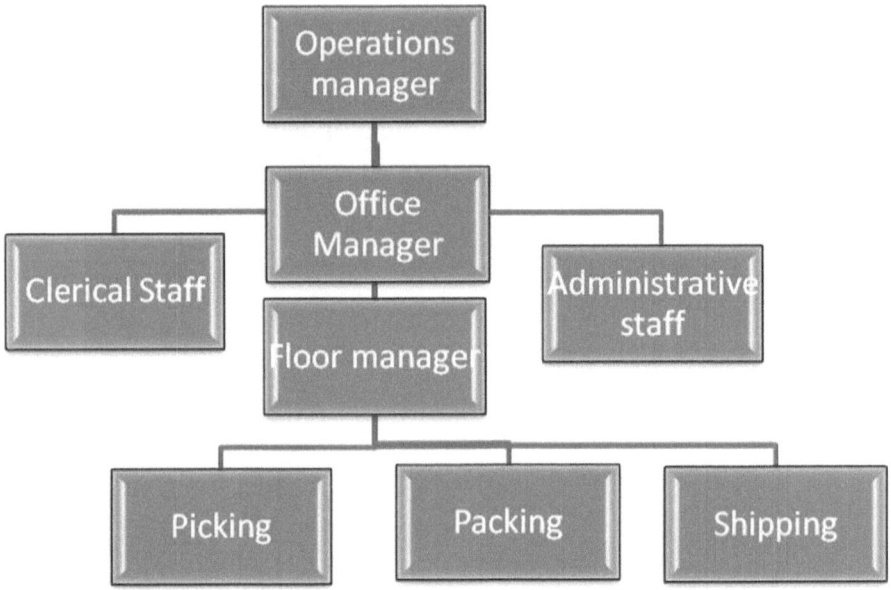

Leadership and Management

The discussion of the organization chart is a good segue into the leadership and management discussion. It is important for small-business owners to be able to differentiate between a leader and a manager. Establish which roles you want to be as the business owner and ensure that you are trained to perform the functions. Being the boss does not imply functionality in these roles. Improper leadership and management can destroy a small business. In essence, a leader should be principle oriented while a manager is process oriented as far as the business functionality is concerned.

A manager is activity oriented and manages processes, which may include the administration and supervision of the performance of those processes by personnel. The management role involves defined objectives and processes. Peter Drucker (1909-2005) stated that management's most basic functions were those of marketing and innovation.

A leader is principle oriented and is focused on the people. His role involves vision and establishment of an organizational culture directed by the mission statement and vision of the company. He is responsible for ensuring that personnel are informed and knowledgeable about the business's goals and mission. A leader's role is to ensure direction toward the company mission and to step up in times of crisis (BusinessDictionary.com).

ETHICS

Throughout business ownership and management, there exists a catalyst called ethics. More universities are implementing ethics today into their course structures for business instead of a stand-alone that usually comes in your freshman year, and there is no question about the reason: Enron, IRS, Walmart, financial institutions, and small-business owners are all feeling the pinch these days due to unethical practice.

You may recall the multimillion-dollar lawsuit brought against McDonald's a few years ago, because hot coffee spilled from one of their cups onto a customer and there were no indications on the cup that the contents were hot. Or just look at the housing market if you want a more solid, large-scale example.

When do companies decide to take avenues around the ethical steps? It's when money becomes the goal. The goal in business is not to make money—that's the *mission*. The goal is to provide quality product and service to attain customer satisfaction, thereby adding value for the customer; by doing so, the mission of making money will be achieved. Keep in mind when you read the previous statement that we are discussing the topic of ethics as a stand-alone.

Making money became the focus point of *all* the examples listed above. What went wrong? While the market became more and more saturated and market share dropped, instead of companies trying to think their way out of situations, they found it easier to cut corners, breach compliance, and throw the rules and regulations of proper practice to their backs. Don't spend money on ethical review—it takes away from productivity, it slows things down, and it provides a roadblock in productivity flow. In reality, it saves you money and adds value to your product or service. Consider why large businesses perform internal and external audits.

No matter how good that McDonald's cup of coffee was, it was not meant to be worn, and a label on the cup would have sent that message. Now there are the skeptics that would say, "Well, didn't the customer know that the hot coffee they ordered would be hot?" As the business owner, you *must* do what is necessary to protect your business, reputation, and product and leave that type of rationale alone. This is not to sound redundant, but the ethics of the business owner to do what is right turns into ethical business practice, which, in turn, protects the business.

In the end, wouldn't you say that ethics is a cost component and worth the investment?

A simple example of personal ethical or compliance breach that turns costly would be a quarter ($0.25) in the parking meter for fifteen minutes, but you're running out to the store for "two minutes" only to take the chance and find the ticket slip securely under your wiper blade for $25.00.

Scope of Ethics

There are ethical aspects in all areas of business, from employer/employee to negotiation and contracting. For example, is it okay to hire a contractor as an independent contractor and then assign hours and treat them as if they were any of the other managed employees? The answer is no, and there are laws that define an independent contractor from an employee. Breach of this law can lead to you having to provide the same benefits to this individual as you would other employees.

In negotiation, it's every side of the table for himself, isn't it? So how does ethics play into this battleground? One example is the "truth in negotiation" form, where you basically sign and assure the other party that you are being honest. Breach of this would render the ensuing contract null and void. Also, there are nondisclosure forms that an entity negotiating with multiple potential candidates should sign and many more aspects that the small-business owner should be aware of when entering into negotiations, especially with larger entities.

Employer/employee relations are very-high-percentage areas for ethical breach. There are the obvious workplace taboos, but what about the *unwritten* ethical breaches that are seemingly more of a business decision? For example, paying way below the market rate or promoting a high-paying client's relative over a qualified and more deserving employee or blaming your employees or favoritism.

A business owner should be aware of how dangerous it can become to be part of his operation, especially when there are other employees involved; and from the hiring process, he needs to present an organization compliance document that clearly outlines the parameters and the remedies of compliance. Most of all, he needs to keep himself at a respectable and honorable position if he is to have an efficiently running operation. It is imperative that he understands that his actions in his role as leader and manager will influence the staff regardless of what is written in company policy, manuals, etc.

The ethics of a small-business owner is vital to his business's success. I have advised business owners with employee problems who do not have the leadership or management skill to remain separate from their employee operations, and they have explained that they are in the operation to save money. When I get into this discussion, it is clear that they do not understand that, from an ethics standpoint, if they are not going to take that leadership and management responsibility seriously, then they will never get the full potential of their employees. It is difficult to mediate and resolve employee issues when, for example, you clearly demonstrate favoritism or openly detest disgruntled customers or other acts that diminish your status as the business owner.

Communication is a vital part of business success. This topic is placed under ethics because it is imperative for the small-business owner to understand that communication is the lifeblood of his business. By not implementing proper communication channels and processes, he is actually being unethical to the success of his business. All levels of employees and management should be given unintimidated opportunities to voice their opinions in an ethical manner. These communication freedoms are essential for process improvement. The small-business owner needs to remember that others may see process improvement opportunities or impediments that, from the small-business owner's perch, would go unnoticed.

Tools of Ethics

There are many tools that a business owner can implement to promote ethics. Ethics assists greatly in organizational culture and promotes uniformity. Along these lines, think about a mission statement, "company goals" manual, motivational signs and meetings, compliance and policy-review meetings, properly implemented communication, and remedies for breach of ethics.

Small-business owners should begin the ethical implementation for internal process by having employees sign a "code of ethics" document at the point of hire. This is not a one-way street though. You must ensure the document is not generic but one derived from your organization's goals and mission.

Proper business-operation documentation and financial record keeping are also good ethical practices. Most important for the small business is the management and leadership ethics. It is important to understand the necessity to establish guidelines throughout the organization. Business owners tend to think that they are above their own law and do not see the ramifications of this mentality.

From an external standpoint, contracts and truth in negotiation documents as well as confidentiality documentations are all good ethical practices. It is easy to market unethically, and today's clients are more in tune with value, so bait and switch, or false advertising tactics, will soon come back to haunt a small-business owner.

One of the key components to a proper ethical strategy that will streamline the business process with the strategy and compliance and regulation is to not look at what others are doing and focus on yourself and the business. I refer to this as the mirror rather than the window view.

Strategy for Small Business

Strategy is the brainwork of the business. A great idea by itself is not worth anything unless there is a good strategy to go along with it. Business strategy is a key component in today's world, and not too many people realize or know the critical fundamental five *W*s and one *H* (who, what, why, when, where, and how) in relation to implementing strategy. We have seen the fundamental five *W*s and one *H* in process application, but in strategy, the fundamental five *W*s and one *H* provide the general outline of what you want to achieve and how you plan on achieving it.

For example, a baseball manager's strategy to lower the hits on his innings can be to walk all the higher-average batsmen, but then from the bigger picture, he allows more loaded bases and places a lot of unnecessary stress on his team. Or he may choose another method that would be more accommodating to the bigger achievement, such as high-percentage pop-up pitches. Whatever he chooses, though, there is no one fail-safe answer. If he starts with defining the problem with *what*, then he asks *why* to add substance to the problem; that is, is it a real problem or a personal desire, etc.? Then he applies *how* and concludes on an approach based on his metrics of the players, etc., and then he moves to *who* and decides whether to pull the guy on the mound or to implement the strategy immediately on the next pitch; and finally, he decides on *when/where* would be the best time to make the move to implement the strategy. It is a simple but thorough thought process, and it can take seconds or minutes, depending on your preparation. After watching *Moneyball*, I assume they have every statistic known to man on the players. The fundamental five *W*s and one *H* can be applied in any arrangement. You have to see how well the application of the questions applies to your specific problem scenario.

Strategy for Success: Risk and Return on Investment

The business entrepreneur, the risk taker, needs to be able to analyze risk and forecast effectively. Process and strategy subcategories such as marketing, sales, and negotiation are essential for promoting efficient avenues of opportunity and success. Ethics plays a key role in these areas as compliance, policy, and procedure if breached can be devastating to a business's reputation, productivity, and revenue.

Risk is inescapable in the business world. However, the balance to risk is the return on investment. Used primarily as a stock-market-investment tool, the "estimated return on investment" formula can be an effective tool to the small-business owner. The caveat here is that you must do your due diligence. You should not pull numbers out of thin air for the estimated return of an investment. There is too much risk involved in decision making as a small-business owner for shortcut applications.

You may utilize the simple formula: (estimated gain from investment – cost of investment) / cost of investment. An example of this tool being effective is that of the purchase of a new property for business expansion. The estimated annual return of that investment is $45,000, and the property costs $150,000. The estimated gain for the next five years is (225,000 – 150,000) / 150,000 = 50 percent return in five years. Therefore, it can be assumed with that rate of return that it will take approximately ten years to *break even* on this investment.

The fundamental understanding that a business owner must grasp is that a strategy is a plan, not necessarily written in stone or fail-safe, and part of strategy planning is to understand that there will be a constant need to return to the drawing board time and time again. It is designed to address where you want to be from where you are currently.

One of the mistakes business owners make is that they fail to see the need to return to the drawing board. They make a decision on a specific strategy, and that's it. Whether it brings success or failure, they are sticking with that decision. One of the big mistakes they make along with this *set-in-stone philosophy* that cements them to their decision is that they usually put a lot of money into these initial decisions.

One example of this is a conversation I had with a business owner who had an eating establishment and decided to invest in trifold paper "take one" menus. He ordered menus by the thousands and had them parked in his establishment near the entrance. They were still in the shipping boxes on the pallets, and I asked him one day about them. He explained that he ordered all these menus as part of his marketing plan. But for months they sat in shipping boxes on the pallet near his entrance because *he* didn't have any time to get to them. Meanwhile, he also complained about the overhead of keeping drivers standing around waiting for the next delivery order to come in.

Since then, he explained, some of the things have changed on the menu or became unavailable, and the prices have since increased due to recent raw material increases. So poor process and strategy were now costing him money instead of making him money. He sold his business a few months after that day because of inability to generate income and its demand of his time. In my opinion, he made one of the best products in his market and was sitting on a cash cow. Now the new owners annihilated his recipe, and the business is on a downhill slide. It all started with poor strategy and poor decision making, not just about the menus, but his set-in-stone philosophy also prevented him from thinking outside the box. Sometimes the inability of a small-business owner to realize his business's potential can be the biggest hurdle of all.

The environment changes so frequently today that it would seem rational to have a backup plan or plan *B* ready for rollout just in case.

Andrew Grove stated:

> The best business strategies must steer a course between the inevitable internal pressure for business continuity and the demands of a rapidly changing world. He led Intel to greatness, and first answers the question "what is business strategy?" with a clear distinction between strategic action and strategic plans. He believes that business strategies should not:
>
> • just be statements of intent;
> • come across like a political speech;
> • have concrete meaning only to management;
> • concern themselves with events far in the future or have little relevance to today.
>
> To formulate a basic business strategy, try this as a simple exercise:
>
> • Take a piece of paper and at the bottom, write a brief account of where the business is now.
> • Then at the top, write where you want the business to be in "x" amount of years (you decide the period).
> • Next, in between the two write what you need to do and when you to do it to get from the bottom of the page to the top.

(http://www.thinkingmanagers.com/business-management/
business-strategy.php)

The above extract taken from ThinkingManagers.com provides a simple plan for creating a strategy. However, look at the advice carefully. Simple doesn't seem like an effective strategy planning, does it?

Simple and effective lean process and continuous improvement tools, if implemented properly, can be all the process strategies you need for successful performance; however, there are more dimensions to business strategy than just the process. A business owner is a salesman; regardless of what he does, he is a salesperson. His work, product, availability, access, etc., make him resourceful and of value (or lack of) to his market. Also, a business owner should know how to negotiate. Negotiation is such a technical area in that I can place it anywhere in the four-principle categories of process, strategy, financial intelligence, and ethics, and it will find a home.

One of the most important areas that are impacted by negotiation is strategy. Business owners need to ensure that they negotiate terms and conditions that are compatible with their success strategy. Many small-business owners are going to get opportunities with the big names in their industry, and the negotiation meetings are going to be more like a yes-man meeting. Your character is displayed in your negotiation skill, and that character will transcend your organization. Do not roll over on negotiations and believe that you can perform damage control later on. It is imperative that you show character in these situations.

An example would be your first business loan with a nationally recognized firm. They have reviewed your business plan, and they have agreed to review your application. Now you are sitting in front of the loan officer and the district manager, and it's game time. You know from your financial planning that you can afford to pay up to 10 percent in interest of the desired amount, but you do not desire to pay more than 12 percent; and your personal credit score, which will be considered since you are a new business, is good/excellent. The loan officer tells you that you are approved and makes it sound like they had to conquer Everest to make it happen because you are a new business. Then he drops the gavel about the APR, which is 29 percent. He explains that the APR will not matter if you make more than the minimum payments. You really need the money. What do you do?

I will not go into details about what you should do, but I will refer you to the "Pearls of Wisdom" page of this book and remind you to be cognizant of who the vendor is and who the customer in this scenario is. Keep your focus on your strategy and anticipate that this type of situation will occur, and have a written counteroffer ready to present in a couple of days.

A business strategy should not provide you with a *set-in-stone* agenda; it should be based on the mind-set of continuous improvement, and it should maintain the principles of change. A traditional strategy needs certain elements to stay firm and certain assumptions to be made. In a scientific model whereby performance is continuously gauged by numbers and key productivity indicators, your process should be firm to withstand internal and external stresses yet malleable enough to accommodate a strategy for success, which is to identify and eliminate process waste, improve upon existing performance, and add quality steps and value to your goods and services to continuously raise the bar of your business's competence and performance.

Strength, Weakness, Opportunity, Threat (SWOT)

Small-business strategy should not be viewed as a business strategy but rather as a success strategy that takes dedication, planning, continuous review, and continuous improvement mentality to accomplish. The success strategy needs an organizational culture befitting of its principles in order to succeed. A business strategy implementing a SWOT analysis tool will assist in this decision. The below illustration of a SWOT analysis layout demonstrates the layout of the SWOT to effectively assist the business owner in their strategy. It is effective especially in those instances where a business may be seeking growth avenues to exploit. The opportunities and threats are external while the strengths and weaknesses are internal. However, you may find that an internal process is threatening your ability to grow, and therefore, some of the listed items may be transposed.

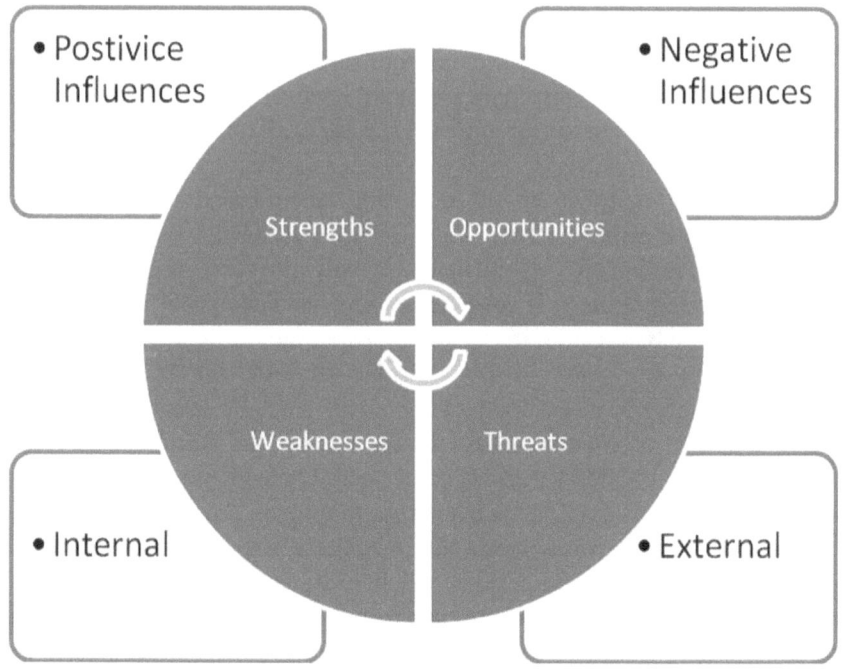

Notice the division of the SWOT analysis. The left-side strengths and weaknesses focus on the internal influences while the right side focuses on the external influences of opportunities and threats. The top half of the analysis layout is directed to the positive components while the lower half is focused on the negative components.

Exploring Marketing Strategy

Business marketing is simply bringing the buyers and sellers together. It is your business's way of saying, "Here we are, and here's what we offer." One of the critical functions for a new business is the marketing strategy. Marketing can be extremely costly but extremely beneficial. Before you begin to market, there are many things to consider. The SWOT analysis is a great tool to identify the considerations when planning a marketing strategy.

Marketing strategies commonly used today are direct marketing whereby you research or invest in a research organization to identify your potential clientele and then you solicit to them directly; guerilla marketing, which makes the assumption of where your potential customers may be and direct marketing in those areas; then there is online marketing and lead generation; traditional marketing such as newspapers, radio, and local chamber of commerce; and other business organization bulletin boards and listings; and how about company marketing through your employees and yourself? Every time you confront a customer, even without saying a word, you are marketing your business. Your business establishment itself is a marketing tool. Ever gone to a filthy restaurant or one with rude staff? How often have you revisited?

Research the many areas of marketing, then based on your SWOT analysis and other reviews of your business niche, identify those avenues that will be most effective to your business. It will not serve that you utilize a national marketing strategy if your service area covers a small county in your state. You may be better off with local newspaper and radio advertising.

New businesses must identify proper strategy for marketing. This strategy is based on your understanding of your business capability. In the initial phases of your business, that is, during the start-up and growth phases, you need to carefully assess your capability with the market that you approach, or you may find yourself wasting money on a market strategy with no realistic return on investment. Many small-business owners direct their marketing against competition rather than to their niche as a new business. Many new businesses have advantages—such as accessibility, affordability, and value—that they do not leverage to their small business's advantage. They make mistakes by attacking larger markets instead of implementing a proper strategy for expansion such as this:

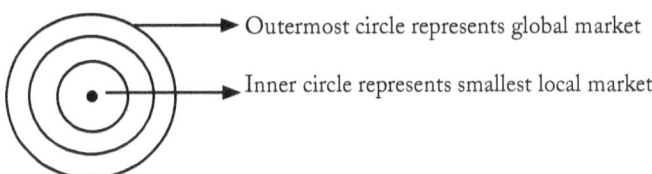

Outermost circle represents global market

Inner circle represents smallest local market

Start with the innermost circle and move outward. Each ring represents a market expansion from a local level, such as city or town, to state to regional to national and even global level. You'll find that this approach is more efficient. Also note that as the marketing approach moves outward, it becomes more expensive. You may be able to implement an initial marketing program for a very small budget, using newspapers, flyers, and traditional marketing approaches from the innermost circle that address your local area. As you branch out, your marketing strategy will begin to increase in cost and address a wider audience. During your business start-up and growth phase, you'll probably want to stay within the inner circles.

Many new businesses rush to establish a website, which I do not disagree with, but if the intent is to garner a large percentage of initial revenue from a website, you'll soon find yourself spending more and more capital to position yourself for recognition on the search engines and not getting the sales traffic that you anticipated. You'll find that you are dangerously competing with words and images that may take precedence over or even misrepresent your actual ability as a small business, so this type of marketing needs to be approached with caution. Your marketing strategy principle must align with your budget and realistic process. A balanced marketing strategy for a start-up business incorporating a mix of various marketing components with proper research to direct your solicitations to your clientele is recommended. This may take a lot of time if you try to do it all by yourself, but sourcing a marketing partner that is affordable will allow you to leverage both the research and the capability you will find resourceful as a start-up. In keeping with the overall principle of this book, it should be emphasized that your marketing strategy should have measurable components to see what works and what is just costing you money without desirable return.

What if you did hit an immediate boom from your marketing strategy as a new business? Would you be able to cope with the volume? Would you be able to provide quality and valuable service to each client?

Financial Intelligence

Simply defined, *financial intelligence* is "gathering the required information needed to understand your capabilities." From a small-business standpoint, we will focus on this topic under two microtopics called business economics and financial analysis.

Why take a social science subject such as economics and pair that with a financial management science subject such as finance? Ironically, it is because of their differences that they are valued as a working pair for the small-business owner or entrepreneur. Finance is directed at money or wealth management, and economics is directed at the production and consumption of goods and services. Now with these definitions and explanations, the impact they can have on the small-business owner begins to become clearer. So in the world of the small-business owner or the entrepreneur, there is value in understanding how both of these elements interact, and there is value in what even a basic understanding of that interaction can bring to your business.

To explain this more directly, the small-business owner needs to understand and assimilate how the internal and external environments affect his revenue flow. The financial analyses are the internal gauges and identifiers of impact, and the understanding of business economics serves to lend light to the small-business owner about the effect specific changes (internal or external) are causing on the revenue of the business.

Let's say for example you were a pizza-shop owner and one of your specialties is eggplant parmesan sandwiches. Depending on climate change, you may anticipate an increase in the price of eggplant (which will become scarce due to the climate change) and, therefore, be able to implement a strategy to rectify that problem. Also, you understand that there is a global shortage of flour and that prices are rising steadily. You may plan a small percentage increase across the board for all your products to compensate *if* you can identify the problem and review the forecasted impact this may have on your figures.

What financial tools can you use to realize the above changes? Your costing sheet, expense report, balance sheet, or income statement may all be able to hint at changes, but you will have to perform the analysis (with your bookkeeper or accountant) to decipher the meaning of the numbers. The underlying issue here is that many small-business owners simply stop at realizing there is an increase in the process and, therefore, simply raise their product cost instead of strategizing an implementation process that will least impact their clients.

Business Economics / Financial Analysis

The business environment has taken a blow as of late due to the global economic crisis. Small businesses facilitate larger ones and provide the lifeblood to the economy. It is imperative that small-business owners understand the impact and influence the economy has on their business, and the key indicators for this impact can be derived from the financial analysis of the business performance. Back to Business 101—the mission is to make money, so if the money is affected, then something is affecting the mission; and if something is affecting the mission, then there must be an area of improvement within the process; and if there is an area of improvement within the process, then there should be a review. This entire process review/ improvement begins with the key productivity indicators derived from financial analysis. From a small-business owner's perspective, unlike a larger entity where the process-improvement process may begin with productivity measurements because the financial effect will not be felt for another quarter, et cetera, in a small business, the financial effect is more immediate.

Business Economics

1. *Business economics* is defined as the study of the financial issues and challenges faced by corporations. Business economics is a field in economics that deals with issues such as business organization, management, expansion and strategy. Studies might include how and why corporations expand, the impact of entrepreneurs, the interactions between corporations and the role of governments in regulation.

   Corporations make strategic decisions that can result in a profit or loss. Business economics studies how and why corporations make these decisions and how other economic factors can influence their choices. (http://www.investopedia.com/terms/b/business-economics.asp)

Although this definition targets corporations, it impacts businesses at all levels and sizes.

2. *Business economics* is defined as the study of how businesses manage scarce resources. (http://www.basiceconomics.info/#sthash.HdvDG zn9.dpuf)

From a microeconomic supply-and-demand perspective, it is vitally important that the small-business owner understands the business economics affecting his particular market and industry in terms of threats and opportunities. Though the definitions above may imply large entities, the impact on the small business is exponentially more than that to larger firms. This is what causes the 50 percent failure rate in start-ups under five years. To venture into this topic requires caution because it can be overwhelming. Here's what the entrepreneur and small-business owner need to understand: how does this affect my operation and my revenue?

We begin to look at things like inflation, availability of resources, and general supply and demand. This is critical for the small-business owner to gauge and respond to change as a measure of cost control and productivity. How a business markets its product and how it identifies and establishes its customer base are dependent on the knowledge of business economics.

Breakeven Analysis

The term *breakeven* was loosely used above in terms of an investment. What is breakeven analysis? The breakeven analysis chart can be used for deriving the point at which your total invested expenses into your product or service will equal to your income derived from that product or service.

For example, if you produce a product that costs (variable and fixed) $500 to make ten units and you sell each unit for $50, then your break-even point for this product will be one unit, so basically, you are simply replacing your cost of making that one unit with the sale of that one unit and not making any profit. If you revise the figures to sell the product for $60/unit and your breakeven remains the same, so your profit margin is now 20 percent. Note that increasing volume also increases variable cost, and it is not going to improve your break-even point. You must find a way to cut cost in process, production strategy, and raw materials or increase the selling price.

Breakeven analysis is a tool that is useful for gauging business performance, but it can be used in a versatile manner. For example, as a technique for pricing your product competitively, using breakeven analysis can be implemented by calculating what your breakeven analysis is in terms of pricing and volume and leverage those findings to find a price point that is below your competitors' yet still enough for you to see a profit margin.

Financial Analysis

Understanding the Tools That Illustrate Assets, Liabilities, Income, Expenses, and Capital and/or Equity

Another important aspect of this two-topic subcategory is that of financial analysis. A business owner must have certain analytical skills in order to make productive decisions. Being able to analyze simple financial reports—such as profit/loss, cash flow, income statement, depreciation, and balance sheets, for example—is critical to identifying hiccups in your operation, overspending, and quality control. Take, for example, employee overtime. Many businesses today implement this activity as a dual benefit to both the employee and the company. Now let's say you are aware of the value of one hour of production in a dollar amount. Let's say, for every one hour at $12 per hour, an employee yields $35 to the business. Now let's say, things got busy and you increased overtime, but an employee takes the extra time to go slow (more of a relaxed pace), which drops his production to yield $12 per hour. How does this affect your business? This is a simple example of how critical it is to understand your figures and know your numbers as the business owner.

Outsourcing accounting, bookkeeping, and payroll is a good practice to ensure all the compliance and proper filing deadlines, etc. However, you should ask for reports to assess your business for yourself and ask your accountant or bookkeeper to assist you in understanding the documents presented to you so that you can make more informed business decisions. Have a private-audit firm review your financial books at least once every three years to ensure that you are meeting all your compliance requirements.

Key reports that you should have some working knowledge of are the balance sheet, which is a snapshot of a company's financial position at a given point in time and reports your financial status on assets/liabilities and equity or the permanent accounts that the business has, and the income statement, which is a summary of the company's revenues and expenses and basically tells you, as the name suggests, the income your business made after deducting the expenses. What, then, is the critical difference between a balance sheet and an income statement? For the small-business owner, you get from the balance sheet a snapshot of a particular fixed point in time, and it will answer the question "How are we positioned financially?" while the income statement covers a period. The income statement gets straight to the point of answering "How much did my business make?" From these two explanations, you may begin to see the value of being able to utilize these reports. Before any of these operational reports, however, it is crucial that you understand the importance of a budget to get started. Without a budget, you will not have a strategic starting point from which to even begin. Unfortunately, most business owners overlook this important requirement and do not approach it with the integrity it deserves, fixing figures to ensure the numbers pan out rather than looking at the reality that the figures lend to.

Another aspect of financial analysis is being able to set an appropriate cost for your goods or services based on your company size, demographic of your client, market rate of your product for your location, etc. (SBA.gov, K. Klein).

THE BALANCED SCORECARD

A balanced scorecard is a performance measurement and reporting system that strikes a balance between financial and nonfinancial measures (Horngren et al. 2007). The balanced scorecard should display summaries derived from your business's key performance indicators (KPI). The key performance indicators should be metrics directed at what's important in terms of your business goals and objectives.

There are many forms and ways to display the balanced scorecard, and a search online will provide you with a multitude of samples. Here are the basic headings you should adopt as a small-business owner for gauging your business health: financial perspective, internal process perspective, learning and growth perspective, and customer perspective. The core of your balanced scorecard is represented by your company's vision and strategy. It is imperative that growth does not only imply volume. Your business needs to grow in many various dimensions.

It is important to understand how much analysis and research you really need as a business owner. With all this information presented in a concentrated form, it may seem as though your business is going to turn into a constant research project, and in some ways, it is if you are to stay in success mode rather than in survival mode. It may seem a bit overwhelming. How much time would you have in your busy day to allocate to these reports, forms, tools, and research activities?

It is up to you to identify the challenges your small business faces and implement the tools needed by identifying the category of the challenge, i.e., process, strategy, financial intelligence, and ethics. Then identify the tools that will engage the problems most effectively and efficiently.

It is imperative that you understand the importance of a team. Even if you are a sole-proprietor operation, you still need a team with which to network to be resourceful, such as your accountant, lawyer, marketer, salesperson, etc. All the ideas are for naught if you cannot get your organization to assimilate and disperse the ideals and principles of your strategy and process effectively.

There are various tools and techniques to engage the business markets of today, but there are fundamental principles that cannot be overlooked or substituted if you are going to succeed—principles that you must establish. If you are a small-business start-up or entrepreneur with the ambitions to start and successfully maintain your business, you must implement and understand simple principles associated with process, strategy, ethics, and business economics / financial analysis.

Apply the simple techniques provided in this book or the research techniques that you feel comfortable utilizing. Do not enter the business world in survival mode; rather, engage in the business world in success mode. This takes a combination of mental preparedness, business planning, preparation, timing, and execution. Also, surround yourself with a good network of support.

Understand what your team represents and means to your business.

I always advise small-business owners that two of your best partners are your attorney and your accountant. Seek their advice and consultation, and do not be afraid to face reality. If it is best to wait awhile or prepare a bit more in anticipation of a business move, such as a process or strategy, then that's where you should start. Create an action plan rather than implement an action. Seek the consultation and training tools from the free resources, but understand that they are usually providing the information at a grandiose level and the integrated technical skill and implementation methodology may not be part of their curriculum. Finally, understand that business is a risk; and all the above pieces of advice, in conjunction with your actions and decisions as a small-business owner, are designed to reduce, not eliminate, risk.

FINAL THOUGHTS

Small-business ownership is a rewarding and prosperous endeavor if proper strategy, process, financial intelligence, and ethics are applied in principle and as operational tools. The small-business owner of today has to realize his position, establish his niche, and secure his market share. He must look at his position as a small-business owner as an advantage and should be able to address the following:

- What is it that I am providing the clientele that wasn't there before?
- If I would cease to exist after a few years, what will this community lose?
- How does my business make this market better?
- Do my clients have value from my services, and how do I plan to improve upon those values in six months, one year, two years, etc.?
- Am I priced right for my client *and* my business?
- Are all my practices, processes, and strategies compliant?
- Do I value my employees? Do I demonstrate this to them?
- Am I happy with my business's performance?
- Where am I as a business owner, and where do I see myself in six months, one year, two years, etc.?
- Is my business built to take me there? What needs improving? Are my metrics aligned with the key performance indicators?

Understand and utilize technology. The Internet has a wealth of resources that the small-business owner does not tap into. Take advantage of local seminars and events promoted by your Chamber of Commerce or Economic Development Office. Do not be afraid to say you've made a mistake, and always have a process and strategy in place for immediate and future goals. Small-business ownership is a study in continuous improvement.

Ensure that your staff and management understand your company goals and mission. And understand that nothing will work right unless there is proper communication. The best ideals, strategy, process, etc., will fail if they cannot be effectively communicated.

You cannot predict the future as a small-business owner, but you can use tools and information currently available to make decisions that can determine the direction of your business's future.

WORKS CITED

Ames, Michael D. and Norval L. Wellsfry. 1983. *Small Business Management*.

Berle, Gustav. 1989. *The Do-It-Yourself Business Book*.

Horngren et al. 2007. *Introduction to Management Accounting*.

http://www.basiceconomics.info/#sthash.HdvDGzn9.dpuf.

http://www.investopedia.com/terms/b/business-economics.asp.

http://www.morebusiness.com.

http://www.qimacros.com.

http://www.thinkingmanagers.com/business-management/business-strategy.php.

Klein, K. "Budgeting Helps Secure Longevity."

Index

www.ingramcontent.com/pod-product-compliance
Lightning Source LLC
Chambersburg PA
CBHW030010190526
45157CB00014B/1945